MESSAGE OF GUADALUPE

by
Gillian Rae

All booklets are published thanks to the generous support of the members of the Catholic Truth Society

CATHOLIC TRUTH SOCIETY
PUBLISHERS TO THE HOLY SEE

CONTENTS

THE QUEEN OF MEXICO

Mexico has more public holidays than any other country in the world, but with the possible exceptions of Christmas and Easter, none is celebrated with more fervour than the feast of Our Lady of Guadalupe.

On 12th December each year, thousands of people gather in or in front of the beautiful basilica in a suburb of Mexico City which is dedicated to the patroness of Mexico. Masses are said, there are processions and displays, and rich and poor alike cross the vast concourse on their knees to seek the blessing of the Virgin.

On this day, all over Mexico, even in the smallest villages, Mexicans honour Our Lady of Guadalupe.

They know her by many names: the Queen of Mexico; 'la Indita', the little Indian lady; 'la Morena de Tepeyac', the dark lady of Tepeyac; or even the familiar 'la Lupita', which, roughly translated, means the little Guadalupe.

Indeed, the deeply Catholic Mexicans are very familiar with their Queen. She is an essential part of the Mexican identity, and her image is everywhere - on the walls of homes and offices, in cars, buses and taxis, roadside shrines, and, of course, on the medals to be found round the necks of young and old.

It is the image of the Blessed Virgin as she appeared at Tepeyac in 1531, with dark skin, Indian features, small, delicate hands clasped in prayer, and sad eyes. Sad, perhaps because the Mexico she came to help was at that time a very troubled country.

Aztecs and Conquistadors

There are many Indian tribes in Mexico - Maya, Toltecs and Zapotecs to name a few.

In the 13th century the Aztec tribe began slowly but surely to conquer the others. By the time the Emperor Montezuma II came to power in 1502, the Aztecs were rulers of a huge empire. But it was still not large enough for Montezuma. From his magnificent capital of Tenochtitlan, later to become Mexico City, he sent his soldiers to conquer the lands of the Mixtec region.

The Aztecs were a proud but cruel people, and they treated those they conquered very harshly, often using them as slaves.

Their religion was a cruel one, too. They worshipped many gods, and made human sacrifices, especially to the god Huitzilopochtli. The tribes of the Mixtec region inflicted two terrible defeats on Montezuma's troops, which led to an increase in sacrifices to appease the 'angry' gods.

It was around this time that Aztec astrologers began to predict that the god Quetzalcoatl, the Plumed Serpent, would shortly appear to put an end to the dreadful bloodshed of war and sacrifices.

Shortly afterwards, in April 1519, the Spaniard Hernan Cortes and his 900 Conquistadors landed on the shores of Mexico. For the Aztec there could be no doubt that Cortes was the incarnation of the Plumed Serpent, and must be appeased.

But Cortes had not come to end the bloodshed. It was to continue for many years to come.

Hernan Cortes was born in the poverty-stricken region of the Estremadura in Spain in 1485. At the age of 19 he left his family to join the army and seek his fortune.

Under the command of Diego Velazquez, he took part in the Spanish invasion of Cuba. It was a brutal struggle which lasted three years, from 1511 to 1514, and cost many lives. Velazquez became governor of Cuba and made Cortes one of his most trusted lieutenants.

The King of Spain at the time, Carlos I, was also King of Sicily, Prince of Flanders and Germanic Emperor. As such he was the ruler of a considerable part of Europe. He was constantly at war, with rebellious subjects, rulers of other lands he wished to conquer, and also with the forces of the Ottoman Empire.

Warfare was very costly and Carlos realised that the legendary riches of the New World could provide him with the means of replenishing his coffers.

He began in the West Indies, then turned his attention to Mexico. On Velazquez's recommendation, Hernan Cortes was chosen to lead the Spanish conquest of

Mexico. Velazquez changed his mind at the last minute, but Cortes was determined to go, and set out sooner than had been planned before Velazquez could detain him.

It must be said that Cortes was bent on conquering Mexico, not so much for God, Spain and the King, but for his own glory and personal enrichment.

Cortes in Mexico

He left Cuba in February 1519, with around nine hundred men, most of them, like himself, from the Estremadura region, 20 horses, and 11 cannon. Two months later, the ships which carried them landed on the Tabasco Coast. They were attacked by the Maya living there, but repulsed them and advanced into the Veracruz region.

A local chieftain, wishing to ingratiate himself with Cortes, offered him the 'gift' of a slave girl. Her name was Malintzin, but the Spanish dubbed her Dona Marina, and she became popularly known as la Malinche. A very intelligent woman, she quickly became indispensable to Cortes. She mastered the Spanish language rapidly and acted as interpreter in the Spaniards' dealings with the natives. To this day her memory is despised by Mexicans, who consider her to have betrayed her race and her country by collaborating so closely with the invaders. The word 'malinchista' is used to denote a traitor.

The Conquistadors were met by ambassadors sent by the Emperor Montezuma. Convinced that Cortes was the incarnation of the god Quetzalcoatl, Montezuma had given instructions that the Spaniards be fêted and showered with gifts. Cortes and his troops were most gratified, but instead of pacifying them, as was the intention, the displays of wealth with which they were confronted only served to increase their greed.

If Cortes was able to conquer Mexico with so few men and weapons, it was only because so many of the non-Aztec tribes allied themselves to the Spanish invaders, hoping to throw off the burden of Aztec domination under which they had laboured for so long. It was with the help of the Totomacs and the Tlaxcaltans that the Conquistadors were able to reach the capital, Tenochtitlan.

Montezuma received them warmly, still under the illusion that Cortes was the god Quetzalcoatl. The Spanish thought they might be able to subdue the people with little difficulty, but they had to make sure they knew that the Spanish were now in control rather than Montezuma. They decided the best course was to take the Emperor prisoner.

At the beginning of the year 1520, Cortes was obliged to leave Tenochtitlan. He had word that Velazquez, angered by Cortes's disobedience in leaving Cuba when he did, had sent another expeditionary force, not only to subdue the Mexicans, but to bring Cortes himself to heel. In his absence, the troops were placed under the

command of Pedro de Alvarado, who was understandably
nervous about this great responsibility.

Rebellion

The Aztec nobility gathered to celebrate a religious festival,
the Toxcalt. Alvarado panicked, thinking it was an uprising,
and ordered their massacre. This sparked off a real
rebellion, and Alvarado eventually ended up besieged in the
Palace of Axayacatl. This was the situation which faced
Cortes when he returned on 24th June.

Three days later, Montezuma, who had been well treated
by his captors and thought the situation could be resolved
by diplomacy and negotiation, appeared in public to try to
put an end to the rebellion. But the people would not listen
to him. Instead, considering him to be a traitor, the more
fanatical resistors of Spanish rule stoned him to death.

Three days later, surrounded on all sides, Cortes and his
men were obliged to withdraw from the city under cover of
darkness. They had to fight their way out, and this night
became known as 'la Noche Triste', the Night of Sadness,
as almost half the Spanish forces were killed.

Cortes and his remaining men regrouped and, with the
help of their non-Aztec allies, they began to lay siege to
Tenochtitlan. They were helped by the fact that an epidemic
of smallpox had broken out in the city. Ironically, this
disease had hitherto been unknown in Mexico, and had in
fact been carried there by the Spanish.

Montezuma had been succeeded by one of his nephews, but he had died of smallpox and another nephew had taken power, 18 year-old Cuauhtemoc, whose name meant 'the eagle who falls'. For almost three months he held out heroically against the Conquistadors, but on 13th August 1521, it was not only the eagle who fell, but his capital too.

The Spanish destroyed the city of Tenochtitlan and rebuilt their own capital, naming it Ciudad Mexico, or Mexico City.

Tenochtitlan had been a splendid city of sophisticated design, home to around 700,000 people. At its heart had stood the great Teocalli, the temple where the Aztecs had worshipped their cruel gods. When Cortes first arrived in the city, Montezuma had taken him by the hand and led him up the 114 steps of the Teocalli, where he proudly showed him the panorama of markets, roads, houses and canals spread out before them. At first, the Spanish could not help but be impressed, but they saw the other side of the coin in the interior of the Teocalli, where the bodies of the victims of human sacrifice lay rotting. Perhaps it was then that they realised the Aztecs could not after all be brought peacefully into submission as they had hoped at first.

The Teocalli was finally razed to the ground and the stones from it were used to construct the magnificent cathedral of San Francisco, to the greater glory of God.

Men of War and Men of God

The Aztec Empire had been destroyed forever, but the bloodshed was not yet over. The capital belonged to the Spanish, and they were well-received in some parts of the country, which they now called New Spain, but they met with resistance from many tribes, notably the Maya. They were not conquered until 1547 at Yucatan, and in fact the interior of their region was to remain independent until the end of the 17th century.

The main aim of the Spanish was the economic exploitation of the country and its people, but they also realised their responsibility to introduce the conquered Indians to the Catholic Faith.

Queen Isabella of Spain held a council with clergymen, theologians and men of law. They reached the conclusion that the Indians did indeed have souls, and therefore it was the duty of the Spanish to convert them. Indians were to be considered free men and subjects of the crown. They also decreed that the Indians were to work for the benefit of the settlers, but that they in turn must guarantee the spiritual and material welfare of their workers. This system was known as encomienda, there was however, a great abuse of it by the Spanish colonists.

There had been a few chaplains with Cortes's original force, but now Cortes wrote to Spain requesting that missionaries be sent over. He specified that, in his opinion, it would be better to send monks or friars, particularly Franciscans and Dominicans, rather than secular priests, as the latter were more likely to be swayed by the riches so easily obtainable in the country and might not always set a good example.

Missionaries in Mexico

So the first missionaries arrived, almost all of them Franciscans or Dominicans, as Cortes had advised.

They set to work with a will. Their first task was to master the native languages, of which there were many, the main one being Nahuatl. They also taught many of the Indians Spanish.

They destroyed the temples and shrines of the old gods and built Catholic churches and monasteries in their place.

Fighting was still going on in many areas, so these buildings were often fortified. As a reflection of the poverty to which the monks were vowed, they were very austere and simple in style, owing more to Gothic and medieval architecture than to the more ornate Renaissance style then current in Europe.

Music played an important part in the religion and lives of the Indians. It was their priests who passed on musical traditions, and the Spanish missionaries, wishing to eliminate all trace of the old religions, decided to encourage the people to learn the music of Christianity rather than paganism.

A mere three years after the fall of Tenochtitlan, the first school of music was founded at Texcoco by a Franciscan, Pedro de Gand. Another Franciscan, Bernardino de Sahagun, translated the Psalmodia Christiana into Nahuatl. A naturally musical people, the Mexican Indians were quick to adopt European sacred music and European musical instruments.

Schools were built, and in 1529 the first university in the Americas was constructed.

The missionaries introduced agricultural techniques which had been unknown in the country, as well as introducing new crops, wheat in particular.

They also treated the sick in the hospitals they built, using techniques which would seem primitive to us now, but which at the time were more advanced than anything previously used in Mexico.

In addition, the friars performed the very important role of protecting the natives from the abuses of the colonists. In spite of the encomienda system, under which they were supposed to be taken care of and educated by their Spanish 'masters', many Indians were in fact being used as slaves.

Soldiers and friars were by no means the only Spanish people in New Spain now. Attracted by the promise of wealth the country had to offer, farmers, artisans, traders and administrators were settling there in droves. Unfortunately, many of them looked upon the native

Mexicans as little better than animals and treated them very harshly. The missionaries could not prevent this entirely, but they did their best. It was a situation which often led to conflict, and many of the friars showed great courage in defying abusive colonists.

If the Indians feared and despised the majority of Spaniards, they were much impressed by the missionaries, and hundreds of thousands of them willingly converted to Catholicism.

The charge often levelled at the friars was that, wishing to convert as many Indians as possible, they gave them only superficial instruction, with the result that many had an incomplete understanding of the Faith, and in fact continued to worship their old gods under new names. This may have happened in a few isolated cases, but generally the missionaries were at great pains to ensure that the Indians had put their old gods behind them when they converted.

Churches and shrines dedicated to Christ or His Holy Mother were often erected in places where a shrine or temple to a pagan god or goddess had been, but the friars were careful that no one should confuse them.

They were very careful in their use of language, too. When giving a potential convert instruction in his native tongue, they never translated the Spanish words for God, the Virgin Mary or a saint into the words which the natives used for their gods and goddesses. They simply

used the Spanish words, to emphasise the fact that
Christianity had nothing to do with the old pagan religions.

Many converts took Spanish names when they
embraced the Faith. One of these was St Juan Diego, who
was to be singled out to carry a very important message
to Mexico and to the world.

OUR LADY AND ST JUAN DIEGO

In 1531 St Juan Diego was 57 years old. He was a convert to the Catholic Faith, and his religion had sustained him in his sorrow when his wife had passed away two years previously.

They had no children and Juan Diego lived with his old uncle. This uncle was also a convert, and had taken the name Juan Bernardino.

They lived in a village called Tulpetlac, some miles north of Mexico City. Their nearest church was quite a distance away, but it was a walk Juan Diego always undertook willingly. On Saturday, 9th December 1531, he was on his way to Mass. Unfortunately, his uncle could not accompany him, as he was in poor health. The 9th December was the date on which the feast of the Immaculate Conception was celebrated in Spain and its colonies.

All alone on the path, Juan Diego thought he heard music, a choir singing a beautiful song which seemed somehow unearthly. Then he heard a voice calling his name, quite distinctly. Surprised and curious, Juan Diego climbed a hill to see who could be calling him. There he saw a radiant young woman, an Indian who appeared to be around 16 years of age. Although the sun had not yet risen, she was bathed in light.

Juan Diego couldn't help but be startled, but any fear he might have felt soon disappeared when the young woman spoke to him in gentle tones. She spoke in Nahuatl, Juan Diego's native language, and asked him where he was going. He replied that he was hurrying to Holy Mass.

"Son", she told him, "I am Mary, the Mother of Our Lord."

When he heard these words, Juan Diego fell to his knees before her. The Blessed Virgin went on to tell him that she wished to help his people and all who sincerely turned to her for help, and that she wished a church to be built on the spot where they now stood, a hill called Tepeyac.

"Go to the Bishop in the city and tell him all you have seen and heard," she instructed him.

Juan Diego, overcome with emotion, promised to do as she asked.

Our Lady left him and he set out for Mexico City. He was determined to fulfil his promise to the Holy Mother, but was nonetheless very apprehensive as to how he would be received by the Bishop. After all, he was only an illiterate Indian worker.

The Bishop was a Dominican named Juan de Zummarraga. He received Juan Diego kindly. The Bishop could not speak Nahuatl and Juan Diego had not yet mastered the Spanish language, so their conversation was conducted through an interpreter, a certain Father Juan

Gonzalez, who was later to publish his testimony recounting all that he had seen and heard during Juan Diego's interviews with the Bishop.

Zummarraga listened attentively to Juan Diego's story of his meeting with the Virgin, and her request that a church be built at Tepeyac. He was impressed by the Indian convert's sincerity, but couldn't imagine why Our Lady would want a church built in such a deserted spot. All in all, he was not convinced. He told Juan Diego that what he had to say was very interesting, but that he would have to think things over. Thus, Juan Diego was gently, but firmly dismissed.

The Second Apparition

It was sunset when Juan Diego reached the little hill at Tepeyac on his homeward journey. He was tired, hungry, and above all, feeling very guilty that he had not been convincing enough and failed in his promise to the Virgin. However, when he reached the top of the hill, the Queen of Heaven was waiting for him. He fell on his knees before her, all his troubles forgotten in her presence.

He told her what had happened during his visit to the Bishop and begged her forgiveness for having failed. He said that she ought to find someone more suited to the task than himself. Mary reassured him.

"My son," she said, "it is you I have chosen. Go back to the Bishop tomorrow, say you have seen me again, and repeat my request."

Juan Diego replied that he was not at all sure if the Bishop would listen to him, but he would certainly do as he was bid, and would come back to the hill at Tepeyac the following evening to tell the Blessed Virgin the results of his second visit to Bishop Zummarraga.

The next day was a Sunday, so Juan Diego went to Mass in the morning as usual. Then he set off once again to walk to Mexico City to see the Bishop.

He did as Our Lady had asked and said that he had seen her again, and that she told him to come back and repeat the request that a church be built at Tepeyac.

The Bishop was still not entirely convinced, but he had taken a liking to Juan Diego and was touched by his piety.

"I'm sure you understand why I cannot build a church just on what you have told me. When you see the Blessed Virgin again, ask her to give me a sign directly from herself, an unmistakable sign, and then I will build the church."

The Third Apparition

Again, Juan Diego found the Mother of God waiting for him at the hill of Tepeyac. He knelt before her and repeated what the Bishop had said. Mary told him to come back the following day at dawn and she would give him a sign to take to the Bishop, one which would convince him of the truth of what Juan Diego said.

Juan Diego bade Our Lady farewell, and promised to come back the following morning. All his doubts about himself had gone. He was sure that the Holy Mother would help him carry out the mission she had entrusted him with.

However, when Juan Diego reached home that evening he found his uncle very ill indeed with fever. He prepared medicine for him and sat up with him all night. When daybreak approached, he felt he could not leave his uncle alone to go to meet the Virgin as arranged. He was sure she would understand the reason for his absence. All next day he cared for his uncle, then on Tuesday morning, Juan Bernardino, fearing that the end was near, asked him to go to fetch a priest to administer the last Sacraments.

The Fourth Apparition

On his way to fetch the priest, Our Lady appeared to him again. He explained why he hadn't come to see her at dawn the previous day, and asked her to excuse him, as he was in a great hurry to get the priest for his sick uncle.

The Virgin Mary told him that he had nothing to worry about, as she had already cured Juan Bernardino. She asked him to go to the top of the hill and gather the roses which were growing there.

Juan Diego was confused. He was so happy to think that his uncle could be cured so quickly. He was also wondering how roses could possibly be growing on top of the hill. They did not usually grow there, and anyway, it was the month of December, when no roses were to be found anywhere.

When he reached the top of the hill, however, he saw dozens of beautiful red roses, dripping with dew, amongst the frost-covered cactus and rocks.

Like most Indians, Juan Diego wore a working apron, called a tilma. It was made of coarse fabric and was large enough to be used as a sort of cloak. He filled the tilma with the sweet-smelling roses and took them back to the Virgin Mary, who took them and rearranged them with her own hands. Then she tied the lower corners of the tilma behind Juan Diego's neck, covering the roses.

"My son", said Our Lady, "this is my sign for the Bishop. Don't let anyone see what you have in the tilma until you are before the Bishop himself. Tell him I made your uncle well again, and that I myself arranged the roses like this. He will believe you, you'll see".

Bishop Zummarraga received Juan Diego for the third time. He may have had an inkling that he was really going to see the sign he had asked for, as, in addition to the interpreter, he called in several more witnesses.

Juan Diego told him what the Virgin had said, then he untied his tilma. The beautiful roses fell to his feet around him, spreading their fragrance throughout the room. Then Juan Diego looked down at the front of his tilma and saw that the Blessed Virgin had left there a sign more beautiful and wondrous by far than the roses. There, imprinted on the coarse cloth, was an image of the Mother of Our Lord in all her glory, just as he had seen her.

The Bishop and everyone else in the room fell to their knees. They were overcome with awe. It was obvious to them all that everything Juan Diego had said had been the truth.

The Church is Built

Filled with joy and wonder, Bishop Zummarraga took the tilma from Juan Diego and reverently carried it into his own chapel, where, with great care, he attached it to the wall next to the altar.

It was not long before news of the miraculous image spread, and the next day a great crowd had gathered outside the Bishop's residence. It was decided to put the tilma on display in the Cathedral, where everyone would be able to see it. Quite a procession accompanied the Bishop and Juan Diego on the way to the Cathedral. The tilma was duly attached to the wall there, and soon the Cathedral was filled with people coming to see the sign Our Lady had given, and to pray to her.

The Spanish priests and monks were, of course, thrilled, and realised that Our Lady's special gift would help them greatly in their work of converting the Indians. The Indian converts, for their part, knew that the Mother of God had not forgotten them in their need, and was there to give them her assistance in their lives which were often full of suffering and troubles due to the harsh treatment of their Spanish 'masters'.

The Bishop felt that the Virgin should be obeyed as soon as possible, and asked Juan Diego to show him and his companions the hill where she wanted the church to be built.

Juan Diego did so, and then they went to see his uncle. He was in perfect health, as Juan Diego had known he would be from what Our Lady had told him. He told his uncle the story of his meetings with the Holy Virgin and the appearance of the image on the tilma. Juan Bernardino had a story to tell, too.

He had been lying in great distress, tossing and turning with a high fever. His one hope was that his nephew would return with the priest in time, that he might make his peace with God and receive the Sacraments. Suddenly, the room was filled with a soft light. He opened his eyes and saw a beautiful young woman standing beside him.

In Nahuatl, she told him of her meetings with Juan Diego and how she had put the picture of herself on his tilma. She told him that she and her picture were to be called Our Lady of the serpent who is crushed. Then she left him and he felt the fever go and health return to him. He had eagerly awaited his nephew's coming. In the Nahuatl language the word for the serpent who is crushed is coatlaxopeuh, pronounced 'quatlasupe'. The Spaniards present whose knowledge of the language was imperfect thought Juan Bernardino had spoken of Our Lady of Guadalupe. This made perfect sense to them, as Guadalupe was, and still is, the site of a famous Marian shrine in Spain. It seemed right and proper that Our Lady of Guadalupe should have chosen to appear in New Spain.

The Immaculate Conception

The interpreter explained the true meaning of the Nahuatl term, and obvious reference to the Immaculate Conception. It was the serpent who tempted Eve to commit the sin which led to the expulsion from the Garden of Eden. The Blessed Virgin was conceived without the stain of original sin, which is why she is often portrayed crushing a serpent under her feet. However, despite this explanation, the name Our Lady of Guadalupe struck a chord with the Spaniards, so far from their native land, and it is by that name that the picture became known forever more.

When the Indian converts heard that the Blessed Virgin had given instructions that a church was to be built at Tepeyac for them, they flocked to the hill. There were hundreds of volunteers to help build it, and it was completed in just two weeks. Our Lady's wish had been fulfilled.

On 26th December, the sacred image was brought from the Cathedral to the new church in a great procession. Even Hernan Cortes took part.

Most of the Indians were in their own traditional garb, and they were so full of joy after the image of the Virgin was placed in the church that they began to dance and sing. During the dancing, one young Indian stumbled and fell against the spear carried by one of his friends. He suffered a wound in the neck which began to bleed copiously. He collapsed and was losing blood so rapidly he was soon unconscious and near death. Two of his friends carried him to the image of the Virgin of Guadalupe and begged her to help him. Suddenly the young man's eyes opened, the bleeding stopped, and he got to his feet. Our Lady had not betrayed their trust in her, and had saved his life. This was the first miracle due to the intervention of Our Lady of Guadalupe. Many, many more were to follow.

Our Lady and the Mexican Identity

Significantly, the spot where the Blessed Virgin chose to appear to her servant, Juan Diego, had once been the site of a temple to the mother goddess, called Tonantzin. This was where the church was built, a perfect symbol of the casting-off of the old pagan religions of the Mexican Indians and the embracing of the Catholic Faith.

While many Indians had converted, others had stuck to their old ways. While they saw the good being done by the missionaries, they also saw the hard, sometimes barbaric, treatment meted out by the Spaniards to their Indian workers. Such people did not set a good example, being nominally Catholics, but behaving in a way quite contrary to their religion. However, with the appearance of the Virgin Mary to Juan Diego and the miraculous image on view for all to see, a great many of those who had previously been sceptical turned towards Catholicism. They realised that it was not just the white man's religion, but a religion for all, no matter what the colour of their skin or their station in life. After all, was not the Virgin in the picture of the same race as themselves, and had she not chosen to appear to a poor illiterate Indian peasant?

Amongst the Spaniards, though, there were many doubters. There were those, among them even certain churchmen, who thought the whole thing was a 'put-up job' on the part of the Church to win more Indian converts. There were also those whose limited knowledge of what was supposed to be their own religion could not let them imagine that the Virgin Mary could take the appearance of a brown-skinned Indian girl, or that she would bother to appear to someone like Juan Diego. Of course there were, too, those Spaniards whose faith was such that they realised that Our Lady had conferred a special privilege on the country they called New Spain. Most of the clergy, naturally, encouraged devotion to Our Lady of Guadalupe to deepen the faith of the converts, who were led to a greater understanding of God through His Holy Mother.

However, it would be true to say that for a long time Our Lady of Guadalupe was regarded as a particularly Indian devotion. Spaniards tended to turn more towards the Virgin of Los Remedios, whose statue had been brought from Spain to Mexico by Cortes's Conquistadors.

In 1737 there was a terrible outbreak of typhoid in Mexico City and its outskirts. Hundreds died, and it looked as though there was no way to stop the terrible sickness from spreading. It was even feared that it could spread to other parts of the country. Our Lady of Guadalupe was appealed to by the faithful of the city. Masses were said and prayers offered in the Basilica of Our Lady of Guadalupe. Mary is never invoked in vain, and the typhoid epidemic stopped as suddenly as it had started.

Hundreds of miracles had been reported as having been due to the intervention of the Virgin of Guadalupe, but it was because of the ending of the typhoid outbreak that she was officially proclaimed Patroness of New Spain.

Church and State in New Spain

The Catholic Church was a unifying force in New Spain. Its power was second only to that of the King of Spain and his representatives in the colony. In fact, King Carlos III of Spain felt that the Church was becoming rather too powerful. There were stirrings of a desire for independence from Spain, and this desire found some support among the clergy, in particular the Jesuits. Two-thirds of the population were Creoles, that is to say, people of Spanish descent who had been born in the colony. The rest of the population at that time was made up of Spaniards who had been sent out from Spain, Indians, and Mestizos, who were people of mixed race born of unions between Spanish and Indian.

Carlos III decided to expel all the Jesuits from New Spain, a very drastic measure indeed, as so many of them had been born there, and they played a very important part in the administrative, educational and spiritual life of the country.

Carlos's next move, in 1804, was to demand the transfer of the not inconsiderable funds possessed by the Church in New Spain into the coffers of the Spanish Crown. The result was economic chaos, and an ever-increasing number of people calling for independence, which was exactly the opposite of what Carlos had intended.

In 1808 Napoleon Bonaparte invaded Spain, obliged the King to abdicate, and put his own brother, Joseph Bonaparte, on the throne, proclaiming him King of Spain and all her colonies. Spanish control over Mexico became tenuous, to say the least, although many remained loyal to the deposed king.

The Fight for Mexican Independence

On 10th September 1810, Miguel Hidalgo y Costilla, a Creole priest in the parish of Dolores, approximately 130 miles away from Mexico City, launched a call to rebellion against the Spanish, which became known as the *Grito de Dolores*. Six days later, a group of rebels, under Hidalgo y Costilla and a nationalist army captain named Ignacio Allende, launched the first armed uprising. Their battle-cry was "Long live the Americas! Down with the evil government! Long live Our Lady of Guadalupe!"

Our Lady of Guadalupe had become so identified with the country that her name was used as a rallying-cry for those who wished independence from Spain. The nationalists even fought under a banner bearing her image. For them, the Virgin of Guadalupe represented Mexico, as opposed to colonial New Spain.

The royalists fought under a banner which bore the image of the Virgin of Los Remedios, the 'Spanish' Virgin. Each side was convinced that 'their' Virgin would help them to victory, apparently not realising that Our Lady of Guadalupe and the Virgin of Los Remedios were of course one and the same. They did not seem to realise either that the image of the Mother of the Prince of Peace was perhaps inappropriate on a banner which would lead men into battle to fight and kill one another.

The fight for independence was to be a long and bitter one. It was not until 1836 that Spain finally recognised the independence of Mexico. But the fighting was not over. The nineteenth century was a very troubled one for Mexico, with internal conflicts, a war against the United States, a conflict with France and another with Austria. The early twentieth century was to see a revolution led by Pancho Villa and Emiliano Zapata. Internal power struggles and political instability caused a great divide between the wealthy minority and the majority of Mexicans, most of whom live in poverty. It was only in the 1990s that there began to be a glimmer of hope that Mexico could become a prosperous, democratic nation.

Although one of the leaders of the original independence movement was a priest, Miguel Hidalgo y Costilla, the persecution of the Church begun by Carlos III did not end with independence. On the contrary, Mexican leaders of all political persuasions feared the power and the influence of the Church, and terrible restrictions were placed on the rights of the clergy. For example, they were not allowed to run Catholic schools. Most of these restrictions were lifted around 1940, but Mexico still officially did not recognise the Vatican until the early 1990s, when relations were re-established by President Carlos Salinas, who realised what an important role the Catholic Church played in his country.

For many years, Mexico was one of the most fiercely secular states in the world, but, paradoxically, the Mexican people were among the most devoutly Catholic in the world. Throughout all the turmoil, there was very little falling-away from the Faith. This can largely be attributed to the devotion Mexicans have always had to Our Lady of Guadalupe.

No government actually went so far as to prohibit Catholic worship, no doubt fearing a popular uprising.

However, in 1921 anti-clerical fanatics placed a bomb under the image of Our Lady of Guadalupe in the Basilica. It exploded during High Mass, but not only was no one injured, the picture itself was completely untouched by the blast.

The only damage was to a Crucifix which was bent out of shape. It can still be seen in the Basilica Museum.

Our Lady of Guadalupe has been the one great unifying factor in Mexico. She has been revered by Mexicans of all races and political persuasions for so many years that she can truly be said to have become a symbol of the Mexican nation. She is honoured throughout the Americas, and was also declared Patroness of the Philippines by Pope Pius XI in 1935.

On the Feast Day of Our Lady of Guadalupe on 12th December, hundreds of thousands of Mexicans come to the Basilica. They come from all over Mexico, and also from other countries. Rich and poor, Creoles, Mestizos and Indians are united in their veneration of the Mother of God, all distinctions forgotten, equal in the sight of God.

THE SHRINE OF OUR LADY OF GUADALUPE

The church built by Indian volunteers in 1531 housed the image of Our Lady of Guadalupe until 1709. For a good number of years it had been clear that the original church was too small to accommodate all the pilgrims who came there, and that the building itself, having been hurriedly constructed, would not last forever.

In 1709 the sacred image was moved to a new basilica, built at the foot of the hill of Tepeyac. It is a huge, ornate building, built in the architectural style of the times. The interior is perhaps more surprising than the exterior, offering as it does a striking contrast between white marble and gold ornamentation. In front of it is an immense square, often crossed by pilgrims on their knees.

Unfortunately, the basilica was built on rather loose earth. By the 1960s it had started to sink and was showing signs of tilting. It obviously constituted a danger, and the decision was taken to build a new basilica, just beside the old one, on the west side of the square. The architect chosen to design it was Pedro Ramirez Vasquez, who had been the architect of the National Museum of Anthropology. This modern building in Mexico City is considered by many to be one of the most beautiful buildings in the world.

The new Basilica of Our Lady of Guadalupe was inaugurated in 1976. It is a vast, open structure in concrete and

white marble, and can accommodate 20,000 people. What is
unique about the interior is that it contains no statue and no
image other than that of the portrait of Our Lady on Juan
Diego's tilma. This is hung above the main altar. An ingenious
solution was found to prevent overcrowding around the altar
and at the same time to allow pilgrims to see the sacred
picture from as close as possible. Four moving walkways
circle the altar at the level of the image. It is certainly a
surprising sight to see in a church, but it is extremely practical.

The basilica is often full to capacity, and to hear
20,000 voices raised in praise of the Lord during Mass is
an impressive experience.

Beside the old basilica is the Capilla del Pocito
(Chapel of the Fountain), which dates from the end of
the 18th century. The dome of this building is covered
with beautiful blue and white tiles, of the kind known as
azulejos. Inside there is a spring, the waters of which are
said to have miraculous properties. Many visitors to the
basilica come here to collect water from this spring.

The back of the old basilica has been converted into
the Museum of the Basilica of Guadalupe. On display
here are treasures from the old basilica, and a wonderful
collection of offerings left by pilgrims. Many of these
take the form of retablos, little squares of iron or silver
painted by the donors. Most are in thanksgiving for
graces received through the intervention of Our Lady, and
many are very touching in their simplicity and sincerity.

Stairs behind the old basilica lead up to the top of the hill, where stands the Capilla del Cerrito (Chapel of the Hill). It marks the precise spot where Our Lady first appeared to Juan Diego. The chapel dates back to the 17th century.

From there, stairs go down the side of the hill to the Jardin del Tepeyac (Garden of Tepeyac) where there is a monument called La Ofrenda. This is built in a modern style and represents the Virgin of Guadalupe receiving offerings from several Mexican Indians and a Spanish priest.

From the garden a path leads down to the main square, passing the Capilla de Indios (Chapel of the Indians). This dates from the 17th century, but was built on the spot where Juan Diego lived from 1531 until his death in 1548. A little house was built for Juan Diego and his uncle to live in, and during the 17 years that he stayed there, Juan Diego must have told the story of his meetings with the Blessed Virgin many times over to pilgrims who came to meet him.

In 1531 the hill of Tepeyac was a deserted spot some miles away from Mexico City, but now it forms part of the outskirts of this enormous metropolis, which is one of the most densely populated cities in the world. There are many buses which go to the basilicas, and even the underground will take the visitor there. In fact, there is an underground station called 'Basilica'.

The shrine of Our Lady of Guadalupe has been for centuries, and still is today, the greatest centre of pilgrimage in the Americas.

POPE JOHN PAUL II IN MEXICO

Pope John Paul II made more than one visit to Mexico, but his first was in January 1979, only a few months after becoming the first non-Italian Pope for centuries.

He was the first Pope to have travelled widely outside Italy. He was warmly welcomed in all the lands he visited, but the enthusiasm with which he was greeted in Mexico has rarely been equalled elsewhere.

The visit took place in a rather delicate situation, as Mexico was a secular state, officially recognising neither the Vatican nor the authority of the Church. However, the President of the Republic of Mexico was at the airport to greet John Paul on his arrival in Mexico City. If his welcome to the Pope was cordial and no more, the crowds which lined the streets were wild with joy. The bells of all the churches in the city sounded peals of welcome to the Sovereign Pontiff.

Mexico was facing a great many problems at that time, political and economic instability among them. Many priests in Mexico, and indeed all over Central and South America, had turned away from the traditional practices of the Church, seeking instead the solution to the nations' problems in radical politics.

John Paul II's objectives in Mexico were to reinforce the faith of the population in general, but also that of the often errant clergy, and if possible to help relax the restrictions placed on the Church by what was at that time one of the most anti-clerical constitutions in the world.

To help him achieve these objectives, he naturally turned to Our Lady. John Paul's devotion to the Blessed Virgin is well known, and he visited most of the most important Marian shrines in the world, beginning of course with the famous Black Virgin of Czestochowa in his native Poland. Needless to say, his visit to Mexico would not have been complete without a pilgrimage to the shrine of Our Lady of Guadalupe.

On the morning of Saturday, 27th January 1979, there was a tremendous heatwave in Mexico City. Despite the temperature, literally millions of people had been gathering all through the night along the 14 mile stretch of road which led from the Apostolic Delegation, where the Pope was staying, to the Basilica of Our Lady of Guadalupe.

The day was to be an emotional one. Hundreds of thousands of people were waiting for his arrival in the square in front of the two basilicas, the old baroque one and the new sombrero-shaped basilica, inaugurated less than three years previously. It was in the latter than John Paul took his seat beneath the miraculous image of Our Lady of Guadalupe, la Morenita.

Pilgrimage to the Basilica of Our Lady of Guadalupe

After traditional hymns to Mary had been sung, the Pope gave his sermon, surely one of the most beautiful he had ever given. Hearing this sermon it was hard not to remember that John Paul II, when he was still Karol Wojtyla, had been a poet of some renown. The sermon was poetic, a poem of love, gratitude and devotion to the Mother of Our Lord.

"Hail Mary! It is with great love and deep respect that I pronounce these words at once so simple and so marvellous! No one can ever greet you in a better way than did the Archangel on the day of the Annunciation. *Ave Maria*, *gratia plena*, *Dominus tecum*.

"I repeat these words which are held in so many hearts and pronounced by so many lips all over the world. Hail Mary, Mother of God."

In his prayer to the Blessed Virgin he asked her help in seeing and teaching the truth, and to meet the future with renewed hope and faith.

In his discourse that afternoon in the same basilica to a congregation of priests and religious, he could not have made himself clearer. He exhorted them to change the injustices and suffering they saw around them through adherence to the truths of the Catholic Faith.

"Be priests and religious," he told them. "Do not be social or political leaders or civil servants of a temporal power." He reminded them of their ecclesiastical commitment and the importance of prayer.

Popular manifestations of Marian devotion are sometimes dismissed by the more 'sophisticated' as not being far off mere superstition, but Pope John Paul II recognised that devotion to the Virgin Mary will lead us to a greater knowledge and love of God. We go through Mary to Christ. There is no need to be highly educated to love and serve God, and Our Lady showed this at Tepeyac when she appeared to Juan Diego all those years ago.

This was reflected in John Paul II's prayer: "Virgin of Guadalupe, Mother of the Americas, we pray to you for all the Bishops, that they may lead the faithful along the paths of intense Christian life, of love and humble service of God and souls.

"Look upon this great harvest, and intercede with the Lord that He may give a hunger for holiness to the whole people of God, and grant many vocations of priests and religious, strong in the Faith, and zealous dispensers of God's mysteries.

"Grant to our homes the grace of loving and respecting life in its beginnings, with the same love with which you conceived in your womb the life of the Son of God.

"Blessed Virgin Mary, Mother of Fair Love, protect our families, so that they may always be united, and bless the upbringing of our children.

"Our Hope, look upon us with compassion, teach us to go continually to Jesus and, if we fall, help us to rise again, to return to Him, by means of the confession of our faults and sins in the Sacrament of Penance, which gives peace to the soul.

"We beg you to grant us a great love for the holy Sacraments, which are the signs of the grace that your Son left us on earth.

"Most Holy Mother, with the peace of God in our conscience, with our hearts free from evil and hatred, we will be able to bring to all true joy and true peace, which comes to us from your Son, our Lord Jesus Christ, who, with God the Father and the Holy Spirit, lives and reigns for ever and ever. Amen."

(For the full text of Pope John Paul II's prayer turn to the back of this booklet).

In 1990, Juan Diego was beatified and John Paul went once more to the Basilica. Again, he knelt before the image of she whom he called "the Star of Evangelisation".

In 1992, at the Pope's request, a chapel dedicated to Our Lady of Guadalupe was established in St Peter's in Rome.

In 2002, Juan Diego was canonised by John Paul II, again in the Basilica.

There are chapels to the Virgin of Guadalupe in many churches and cathedrals around the world, including one in Notre Dame Cathedral in Paris, which was a gift from the Mexican Community in France.

THE IMAGE ON THE TILMA

Our Lady made the roses bloom in December on a hillside in Mexico, but, more wonderful than this, the image of the Mystic Rose herself was found imprinted in all her beauty on the rough fabric of an Indian peasant's apron.

This very image can be seen to this day above the main altar in the Basilica of Our Lady of Guadalupe. We can see exactly how she appeared to St Juan Diego on that day in 1531.

We see a radiant young girl, with the features of a Mexican Indian. Her skin is light brown in colour, which had led to her being called familiarly 'la Morenita', the little brown Lady. She wears a robe of pink, with a faint gold pattern. Covering her black hair, her shoulders, and falling to the ground, is a mantle of deep blue, edged with gold and decorated with stars of gold.

Her hands are raised, palms together, in an attitude of prayer.

The Virgin is surrounded by a radiant light, reminding us that she is the Mother of the Light of the World, Our Lord Jesus Christ whom she accepted to bear, and so give to the world the Saviour who would lead mankind out of the darkness. At the feet of the Queen of Heaven there is a little angel.

The image of Our Lady from St Juan Diego's tilma.

The Symbolism of the Image

As well as the obvious Christian symbolism in the appearance of Our Lady of Guadalupe, there is a deeper, more obscure symbolism, both for Christians and the Mexican Indians of the time.

While Christians will be reminded of "the woman clothed with the sun" in the Book of Revelation (*Rv* 12:1), who had "the moon under her feet", the rays around the Virgin would have made Mexicans think of their god Huitzilopochtli, whose symbol was the sun's rays, and the god of night, who for them was the moon. Thus they could see from the image on the tilma that God was greater than Huitzilopochtli and that by having the moon under her feet the Virgin Mary was more powerful than darkness itself.

In the images native Mexicans made of their gods, they always portrayed them with their eyes wide open and staring straight ahead, giving them a generally rather frightening look. In the picture on the tilda, Our Lady is looking down kindly, on St Juan Diego and on all humanity. The idea of a merciful and loving god had no place in the Mexican's conception of their deities. The Virgin's benevolent regard must have been both novel and attractive to them.

For Catholics the blueish green colour of Our Lady of Guadalupe's cloak is a symbol of immortality and eternity, but for the Mexican Indians it was the colour

worn by royalty, and the gold edge of the cloak was
something they reserved only for those of the nobility.
Similarly, only royalty could be carried on someone's
shoulders, as Mary is seen here supported by an angel.
On learning that the Virgin Mary was the Queen of
Heaven, they would therefore have been quite
predisposed to believe it.

There is one thing that is quite remarkable, although it
may well have passed unnoticed by anyone at the time of
the apparition of Our Lady to Juan Diego. In the early
1980s, Fr Mario Rojas Sanchez and Dr Juan Homero
Hernandez Illescas made a close study of the stars on the
cloak Our Lady wears. They then did extensive
astronomical research and reached the conclusion that
the stars of the winter solstice before dawn on the
morning of 12th December, 1531, were in exactly the
same configuration as those on the cloak. It is as though
the Queen of Heaven had clothed herself in the
firmament itself.

The image has been on public display constantly since
1531, and yet it is as bright as the day Juan Diego
revealed it to Bishop Zummarraga and his companions.
The detail and colouring of the picture are extraordinary.
Despite the heat and the fact it is over 450 years old, it is
remarkably well-preserved; only the edges of the cloth
seem to be a little the worse for wear, probably as a result
of being moved from place to place.

This image is reproduced (although not always accurately or skilfully, it must be admitted) all over Mexico, indeed all over Central and South America, as well as in the United States, where such cities as Los Angeles have a large Mexican population. This sacred image of Our Blessed Mother has been an inspiration to devotion for millions of people throughout the centuries and no doubt will continue to be so for many centuries to come.

THE MESSAGE OF OUR LADY TO MEXICO AND TO THE WORLD

So why then did the Blessed Virgin choose to appear to St Juan Diego on that day in 1531? She appeared and left proof of her apparition on the tilma so that Mexico and later all of Central and South America should turn from their old pagan religions and find Christ. Surely it was not coincidence that she chose to appear at the very place where once Tonantzin, the mother of the gods, had been worshipped. In doing this she clearly indicated that the old gods and goddesses of the Indians had been false ones, and that the true Faith was the one being taught by the Spanish missionaries.

The Virgin chose to appear to an Indian, herself taking the appearance of an Indian girl to prove that the love of God is universal and knows no boundaries of race, nationality or language. Her message here was two-fold. First, in this way she taught the Indians that Catholicism was for all, and not just for Europeans, and that God loved them and wished them to turn to Him. Secondly, she wanted the Spanish to know that, although they considered themselves the conquerors of the Indian peoples of Mexico, they were in no way superior to them simply because of the colour of their skin and their different culture.

If Our Lady chose to appear to an illiterate peasant rather than to a dignitary of Church or State, this was to demonstrate clearly that temporal power means nothing in the eyes of God, that rich and poor are loved by him equally, and that love and obedience to God's will are more important by far than wealth, status or scholarship.

Mary was also undoubtedly moved by compassion at the sufferings endured by many Indians at the hands of the Spanish. She knows what it is to suffer. Did a sword not pierce her own heart as she stood at the foot the Cross, then held her dead Son in her arms? Mexico in the 16th century was a troubled land in troubled times.

Mary, too, had to respond to the questions which people were asking themselves, and which they have always asked, in every country throughout history. How to deal with this seemingly cruel world? Why was there so much suffering, violence and injustice?

Some respond to these questions by fleeing from the world, cutting themselves off from their fellow human beings, thinking perhaps that if they pretend evil does not exist then it cannot harm them. This is perhaps an understandable reaction, but at the same time it is too much like taking the easy way out. This is not the way of life God calls us to.

Others respond by rebelling, taking up arms and fighting, trying to destroy violence by violence. This anger is perhaps understandable, too, but Our Lord tells us that

"He who lives by the sword will die by the sword". Hatred breeds hatred, violence breeds violence, and instead of destroying evil those who act in this way only serve to increase it.

There is a third reaction, and this was the one proposed by the Pharisees and by many others before and since. This is a blind obedience to law and order, an unquestioning acceptance of the rules and regulations laid down by those who have somehow judged themselves to be superior to their fellow man. The problem with this is that it is often man's laws which are obeyed, and not God's. Blind, unreasoning obedience also reduces people to the state of automatons, rather than people, taking from them the freedom of thought, decision and choice which is God's gift to us.

Mary knew that none of these three attitudes was the correct one. She did not revolt, she did not hide behind the law, she did not hide from the world. She faced reality, knowing that she could never know or explain to others all the mysteries of this world. She did not seek to do so; she simply placed her trust in the Lord in humility and simplicity. She accepted to listen and to receive the light and wisdom which can come only from God.

Her strength came not from violence, revolt or power, but through saying "yes" to God. Open to God's gift, she is the sublime example to us all.

She offers above all, hope for those who trust in God. It was a message which was appropriate for the Mexican Indians at that time, but one which applies to all mankind.

Pope Pius XII prayed: "We are certain that as long as you, Our Lady of Guadalupe, are recognised as Queen and Mother, America and Mexico are saved."

Mary is the Merciful Mother of us all, and those who turn to her in confidence will never be disappointed.

Life Force

In 1991 an exact photographic replica of Our Lady of Guadalupe was blessed by Cardinal Posadas on behalf of the Bishops of Mexico. This photograph was named as a Missionary Image, to call upon the help of the Mother of God in the mission to prevent abortion.

The guardian of the Missionary Image is Fr Daniel S. Lynch of St Alban's, Vermont. He is president of the non-profit making organisation which coordinates the journeys of the image.

There are Guardian teams all over the United States and in many other countries in the world. They ask for visitations of the image. There is often quite a delay between the request and the visitation, as demand is so great, but this gives the teams time to prepare a proper reception for the image. These visitations often take place in churches, of course, and in convents and schools, but also in other places where the Word of God is less often heard, prisons, and abortion clinics. Visitations to such clinics where lives are destroyed in complete legality and impunity, are very important as they serve to show the medical staff and the often desperate women who go to them that there is an alternative. The term 'pro-choice'has come to mean 'pro-abortion', but in fact there is a choice involved: the choice between life or death. In saying 'yes' to God, the Blessed Virgin chose life. She chose to give birth to the Son of God, who gives eternal life to all mankind.

It is not by violent action that hearts can be changed, that people will make the decision to choose life, but by the power of prayer and the intervention of Our Holy Mother.

Since June 1991, the Missionary Image has journeyed from the International Rosary Congress at the National Shrine of the Immaculate Conception through the United States and the world. It has been to every state in the US, to over 1,000 parishes, and to the Caribbean, Ireland, England, Canada, Russia, the Philippines, Japan, Israel, Australia, and even China. The image has been the focus of some of the largest pro-life rosary processions ever held, in particular those in Melbourne, Pittsburgh, Dublin, and Port of Spain in Trinidad.

Irish Bishops credit to Our Lady's intercession, the fact that the proposed amendment to legalise abortion in Ireland was voted down.

The journeying of the Missionary Image of Our Lady of Guadalupe has led to conversions, healings, reconciliations and graces all over. The lives of countless children have been saved.

Many women have changed their minds about abortion, and many who have had abortions have been reconciled to God, who is all-forgiving. Not all women who have their babies aborted do so in a casual manner. Often they are themselves to be pitied - alone, under pressure, ill-advised, perhaps in poor health mentally or physically. These are the women who often suffer terrible remorse afterwards. There is a recognised psychological condition known as post-abortion traumatic stress syndrome, but psychiatric treatment is not enough to heal the wounds. Only reconciliation with God can do that.

Mary leads us to her Son, and to a reverence for life. She can shield and protect unborn children, help lift the terrible burden of guilt from those women who are full of remorse for having had an abortion, and lead others to walk out from under the shadow of death and into the light of the Holy Spirit, the Lord and Giver of life.

PRAYER OF POPE JOHN II

O Immaculate Virgin, Mother of the true God and Mother of the Church, who from this place reveal your clemency and your pity to all those who ask for your protection, hear the prayer that we address to you with filial trust and present it to your Son Jesus, our sole Redeemer.

Mother of Mercy, teacher of hidden and silent sacrifice, to you, who came to meet us sinners, we dedicate on this day all our being and all our love. We also dedicate to you our life, our work, our joys, our infirmities and our sorrows. Grant peace, justice and prosperity to our peoples, for we entrust to your care all that we have and all that we are, Our Lady and Mother. We wish to be entirely yours and to walk with you along the way of complete faithfulness to Jesus Christ in His Church; hold us always with your loving hand.

Virgin of Guadalupe, Mother of the Americas, we pray to you for all the Bishops, that they may lead the faithful along paths of intense Christian life, of love and humble service of God and souls. Contemplate this immense harvest, and intercede with the Lord that He may instil a hunger for holiness in the whole people of God, and grant abundant vocations of priests and religious, strong in the Faith and zealous dispensers of God's mysteries.

Grant to our homes the grace of loving and respecting life in its beginnings, with the same love with which you conceived in your womb the life of the Son of God. Blessed Virgin Mary, protect our families, so that they may be always united, and bless the upbringing of our children.

Our hope, look upon us with compassion, teach us to go continually to Jesus, and if we fall, help us to rise again and return to Him by means of the confession of our faults and sins in the Sacrament of Penance, which gives peace to the soul.

We beg you to grant us a great love for all the holy Sacraments, which are, as it were, the signs that your Son left us on earth.

Thus, Most Holy Mother, with the peace of God on our conscience, with our hearts free from evil and hatred, we will be able to bring to all true joy and true peace, which comes to us from your Son, Our Lord Jesus Christ, who, with God the Father and the Holy Spirit, lives and reigns forever and ever. Amen.

What Happened at Fatima

Adhering faithfully to the memoirs of Sister Lucia, the longest surviving seer, this book follows the events of Fatima: from the first stirrings of the wings in the appearances of the angels before the six apparitions of the Blessed Virgin herself, the deaths of Francisco and Jacinta Marto, the subsequent apparitions to Sister Lucia in Pontevedra and Tuy, the consecration of the world and Russia to the Immaculate Heart, the dissolution of Soviet Communism, to the beatifications of Francisco and Jacinta and the opening of the third part of the secret that Our Lady confided to the children in 1917.

ISBN: 978 1 86082 091 5

CTS Code: D651

Lourdes

Place of Healing and Hope

Lourdes is one of the best known places of pilgrimage in modern Christendom. This is the story of Bernadette Soubirous, the eighteen appearances of the Blessed Virgin Mary to her in 1858, and her life and trials.

In this comprehensive and detailed account, David Baldwin draws out the truly inspirational 'Message of Lourdes' for today: a message of hope, healing, intercession and personal conversion towards a loving Father.

ISBN: 978 1 86082 237 7

CTS Code: D661

Message of Walsingham

The Shrine of Our Lady of Walsingham

The Ancient Shrine of Our Lady of Walsingham, England's national shrine, sits in a tiny village on the north coast of East Anglia. Since 1061 pilgrims have made their way there. Paupers and kings have walked, 'slipperless', the last holy mile. Here Mary is contemplated as Mary of Nazareth, the warm hearted Mother of a family that has her Son as the centre.

Pilgrims leave the 'world' to tread the path to this Shrine, praying for themselves and for others, accompanied by the Word of God. They come in response to a deep felt call to conversion, to look again at Christ, to turn back to him. This booklet is a pilgrim's companion.

ISBN: 978 1 86082 030 4

CTS Code: D646

Has this book helped you?
Spread the word!

@CTSpublishers

/CTSpublishers

ctscatholiccompass.org

Let us know!
marketing@ctsbooks.org
+44 (0)207 640 0042

Learn, love, live your faith.
www.CTSbooks.org